Orangutan
LANGUAGE

Rob Waring, *Series Editor*

HEINLE
CENGAGE Learning™

Australia • Brazil • Japan • Korea • Mexico • Singapore • Spain • United Kingdom • United States

Words to Know

This story is set in the United States. It takes place in the city of Washington, D.C., which is the capital of the United States.

Washington, D.C.

CANADA
Washington, D.C.
UNITED STATES
MEXICO

N
W E
S

A **Orangutans.** Read the paragraph. Then match each word or phrase with the correct definition.

Like humans, orangutans [ɔræŋətænz] are members of the scientific group called 'primates'. Although there are many orangutans in captivity around the world today, there are very few left that live in the wild. If the number of wild orangutans continues to get smaller, the entire species could become extinct. Conservation efforts will be essential in ensuring that this intelligent animal can survive.

1. primate _____	**a.** no longer in existence
	b. a specific group of living things that have similar characteristics
2. in captivity _____	**c.** the protection of plants, animals, or natural areas
3. species _____	**d.** unable to move and act freely; kept in a limited space
4. extinct _____	**e.** any member of the highly developed group of animals that includes humans, apes, monkeys, and others
5. conservation _____	

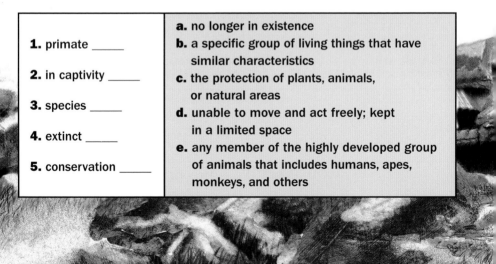

Orangutans in Captivity

B **Orangutan Research.** Read the definitions. Then complete the paragraph with the underlined words.

A coordinator manages a program or an event.
The public refers to the people of a local area, state, or country.
Symbols are signs, marks, pictures, or other objects, that represent something else.
Voluntary means that something is done of one's own will without being forced or paid.

Scientific research is currently being conducted to learn more about how orangutans think and communicate. Rob Shumaker [ʃumeɪkər] is the (1)_____ of the Orangutan Language Project at the National Zoo in Washington, D.C. Shumaker's program is a (2)_____ one in which orangutans can participate if they enjoy it. In the program, Shumaker teaches orangutans to communicate using (3)_____ instead of words. He also invites (4)_____ to come to the zoo to watch the orangutans communicate with humans.

Orangutans are among the most highly developed primates in existence. These unusual animals come from the Southeast Asian countries of Indonesia and Malaysia. They are so much like humans that the word 'orangutan' actually means 'person of the forest' in the Malay language.

The Malay definition is a good one because orangutans are very similar to people in many ways. Orangutans even have the ability to communicate through language, just as humans do. At the National Zoo in Washington, D.C., two orangutans named Inda and Azie are showing the world how well primates can communicate by using language.

 **CD 3, Track 05**

Scan for Information

Scan pages 7 and 8 to answer the questions.

1. What is the purpose of the project at the National Zoo?

2. According to Rob Shumaker, what kind of environment do orangutans need?

3. Why does he believe that choice is so important to orangutans?

Rob Shumaker is the coordinator of the Orangutan Language Project at the zoo. The purpose of the project is to study the orangutans' minds and discover more about how they think. Shumaker talks about the project, and just how much he cares for the orangutans with which he works. "We are really adding to what we understand about orangutan mental ability," he says. He then adds, "I also think that we're doing something very, very good for these individual orangutans." When he talks about them, it is clear that Shumaker has a lot of respect for these animals.

Shumaker believes that orangutans and other apes in captivity need to have a very interesting physical and mental environment; one which **stimulates**[1] them and keeps them happy. To do this, the National Zoo allows its orangutans to move around freely and gives them choices on where they want to go. Even participating in Shumaker's language program is voluntary for them.

Shumaker explains that having choices is very important to these intelligent animals. He says: "It gives the orangutans some choice and some **agency**[2] about what they do day to day. And I think that's incredibly important for a species that has this much **going on mentally**."[3]

---

[1]**stimulate:** increase energy or activity
[2]**agency:** *(unusual use)* responsibility
[3]**going on mentally:** *(slang)* an expression that means 'mental activity'

So how does the National Zoo's language program function? Basically, Shumaker works daily with the orangutans in the program to develop their language skills. Today, he's working at a computer with Inda, a 20-year-old female orangutan. As Inda sits near the screen, she touches certain objects or symbols on it from time to time. "She's just naming the object," Shumaker explains. When Inda identifies objects correctly, she receives a **reward**.[4] Through this process, Inda is learning a vocabulary of symbols that she connects with objects, such as bananas, apples, and cups.

Every day, visitors watch as Shumaker and Inda perform certain exercises on the computer to test what language she knows. Inda is very fast with the symbols—sometimes even faster than the computer! As Inda quickly touches a series of symbols, the computer doesn't respond quickly enough. "Oh, hold on," says Shumaker to the waiting animal, "The computer's not responding quickly enough." He then explains to the people watching her, "but she's doing it correctly," and gently encourages the animal to try again.

---

[4] **reward:** a present for something well done; an award

But is Inda actually using language? Well, not only can she identify food and objects using symbols, but she can also put together the symbols to form simple sentences with a verb and an object. Basically, she can use the symbols in order to get her point across, which is the essential purpose of language.

In addition to their ability to communicate using language, orangutans are like humans in other ways, too. Shumaker **emphasizes**[5] the fact that each orangutan is different in the way it learns, and in the progress that it makes. He points out that they are individuals, and in that way, they are also like humans. "Each one learns their own way. Each one has their own types of questions that they are better or worse at," he explains. He then goes on to add, "The big emphasis is [that] they are individuals, and their progress is not the same as the other orangutans just because [they're all] orangutan[s]."

For example, Inda's brother Azie is not as social as his sister, which means that he doesn't communicate as much. At first, Shumaker thought that Azie was not as intelligent, but that's not true at all. In fact, Azie is a very intelligent orangutan; he just isn't always as interested in communicating with others as his sister is.

---

[5]**emphasize:** put special importance upon

The Orangutan Language Project is part of an **exhibit**[6] at the National Zoo called 'Think Tank'. This exhibit explores the process of thinking and whether or not it is taking place in animals. An interesting aspect of the exhibit is that it actually involves visitors to the zoo in the process. It allows them to observe research on thinking as it takes place.

Lisa Stevens is in charge of the Think Tank exhibit. According to Stevens, one of the most important aspects of Think Tank is that it emphasizes something that people don't usually see—research. She says: "What's really nice about Think Tank is that it brings a lot of the **behind the scenes**[7] activities and research that involve animals **right up front**[8] where [they] should be, where people are going to see [them]."

---

[6]**exhibit:** a show or display at a public place such as a zoo or museum
[7]**behind the scenes:** hidden; not obvious
[8]**right up front:** not hidden; obvious

Zoo officials like Shumaker and Stevens hope that exhibits like Think Tank will educate the public. They also hope that they will increase conservation efforts for orangutans. These interesting animals could become extinct in the wild in the next 10 to 12 years, and they are very much in need of help. Shumaker hopes that people will show more respect to orangutans if they understand how intelligent they are. This, he hopes, will encourage people to protect them better. He explains in his own words: "Give people a chance to know more about what's going on mentally for orangutans. I know that that increases their regard for them!"

Shumaker personally developed the symbols for the orangutans' vocabulary, but he says that the project has really been successful because of Inda and Azie. He explains: "I think of this language project as really a **team effort**[8] between me, and Inda, and Azie. And we all work together on this. It's not my project; it's our project." He then adds: "I want them to voluntarily participate. When they do that, I know that they're doing it because they enjoy it, and they like it, and they want to be involved with it. And that's important."

As Inda and Shumaker continue to work together at the computer, Inda easily identifies a cup by pushing the correct symbol on the screen. Even when Inda makes mistakes, Shumaker carefully guides her to the correct meaning in order to help her development. It's clear to see that both Shumaker and the orangutans enjoy working on the project. That may be why the orangutan language team of Shumaker, Inda, and Azie is such a big success!

What do you think?

1. Do you think the orangutans communicate in the same way that humans communicate?

2. Do you think the language program for orangutans is a good idea?

3. Why or why not?

After You Read

1. In paragraph 1 on page 4, the phrase 'highly developed' means:
   A. threatened
   B. advanced
   C. resourceful
   D. luxurious

2. Who does 'we' refer to on page 7?
   A. orangutans
   B. visitors
   C. researchers
   D. animals

3. What view is expressed by Rob Shumaker on page 7?
   A. His project is the best in the world.
   B. Orangutans are amazing creatures.
   C. All primates work very hard.
   D. Orangutans benefit from his project.

4. According to Shumaker, what makes an environment interesting for orangutans?
   A. choices
   B. people
   C. language
   D. captivity

5. A suitable heading for paragraph 1 on page 11 is:
   A. Orangutan's Falling Vocabulary Level
   B. Inda Successfully Recognizes Symbols
   C. Amazing 20-Year-Old Language Program
   D. Primate Can Only Name Fruits

6. The writer believes that Inda can:
   A. speak sentences in English
   B. only identify food and objects
   C. communicate using language
   D. process verbs faster than Shumaker

7. Which of the following is NOT true about orangutans?
   A. They are individuals.
   B. They are intelligent.
   C. They live in Malaysia.
   D. They progress at the same rate.

8. Azie is _____ as social as his sister Inda.
   A. always
   B. just
   C. not always
   D. usually

9. The purpose of the Think Tank exhibit is to:
   A. let visitors compete with orangutans
   B. explore humans and language use
   C. prove that orangutans are smart
   D. investigate mental activity in animals

10. What effect does Think Tank hope to have?
   A. to make primates better at writing
   B. to teach the whole orangutan species
   C. to involve visitors in research
   D. to protect zoos in the United States

11. Azie and Inda _____ participate in the program.
   A. must
   B. never
   C. voluntarily
   D. unfortunately

12. What's Shumaker's main point in paragraph 1 on page 18?
   A. The orangutans enjoy working with him.
   B. His team of researchers impacts his work greatly.
   C. Inda and Azie only participate once a week.
   D. His symbols are the reason for the project's success.

Honeybee Language
Communication Without Words

Most species of animals have the ability to communicate using forms of language that don't require words or speech. Dogs show their teeth in order to scare other animals. When a cat's hair stands straight up, it is usually frightened or angry. The language of the honeybee (or 'bee') is much more specific. When one type of bee, the worker bee, discovers a food source, it tells other bees about it. It shares the smell of the food and performs a series of dance-like movements. Worker bees use this two-part approach to communicate extremely exact information. They can tell the other bees what type of food is available, the direction in which the food source can be found, and how far away it is.

A Worker Bee

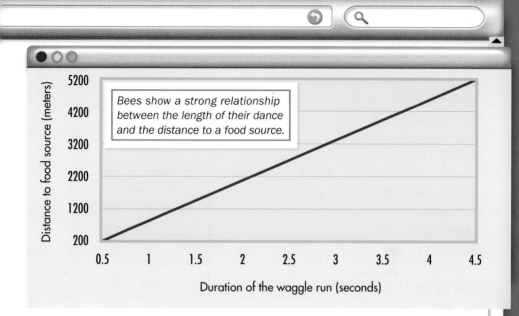

Bees show a strong relationship between the length of their dance and the distance to a food source.

Distance to food source (meters)

5200
4200
3200
2200
1200
200

0.5   1   1.5   2   2.5   3   3.5   4   4.5

Duration of the waggle run (seconds)

When a bee that has been out looking for food returns to the group, it performs one of two dances. This allows it to share information about what it has found. If the food source is nearby (within 50 to 75 meters)*, it does a 'round' dance. This involves running in a small circle to the left first, and then back to the right. The bee repeats this pattern several times. Moving around in a tight circle like this indicates to other bees that the food source is very close.

When the food source is farther than 75 meters away, the bee does what is called a 'waggle' dance. This dance has two parts. First the bee runs straight ahead towards the food source while it 'waggles', or moves its back end. Then, it returns to the starting point and repeats the 'waggle' dance. The length of the waggle portion of the dance tells the other bees how far away the food is. For example, if the bee waggles for 1.5 seconds, the food is approximately 1,400 meters away. If it waggles for 4 seconds, the food is approximately 4,400 meters away. The chart above shows the relationship between the waggle dance length and distance to food.

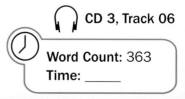

CD 3, Track 06

Word Count: 363
Time: _____

*See page 24 for a metric conversion chart

Vocabulary List

agency (8)
behind the scenes (15)
conservation (2, 16)
coordinator (3, 7)
emphasize (12, 15)
exhibit (15, 16)
extinct (2, 16)
going on mentally (8, 16)
in captivity (2, 8)
primate (2, 4)
the public (3, 16)
reward (11)
right up front (15)
species (2, 8)
stimulate (8)
symbol (3, 11, 12, 18)
team effort (18)
voluntary (3, 8)

Metric Conversion Chart

Area
1 hectare = 2.471 acres

Length
1 centimeter = .394 inches
1 meter = 1.094 yards
1 kilometer = .621 miles

Temperature
0° Celsius = 32° Fahrenheit

Volume
1 liter = 1.057 quarts

Weight
1 gram = .035 ounces
1 kilogram = 2.2 pounds